NAVIGATING THE RELATIONSHIP LANDSCAPE

GABRIELA CASINEANU

Book photos, concept, cover design: Gabriela Casineanu

Cover images: monicore/pixabay.com, presentermedia.com

Editing: Christina Friend-Johnston

Library and Archives Canada Cataloguing in Publication

Casineanu, Gabriela, 1961—, author

Navigating the Relationship Landscape, 1st ed.

ISBN: 978-1-7752390-6-2 (paperback)

ISBN: 978-1-7752390-5-5 (ebook)

DISCLAIMER

The book *Navigating the Relationship Landscape* invites the reader to engage in self-reflection through a combination of photographs and coaching questions.

This book does not replace counseling, professional coaching, or therapy. The information and resources in this book are provided for informational and educational purposes.

Neither the author nor the publisher can be held responsible for the use of the information provided within this book.

CONTENTS

PRAISE FOR NAVIGATING THE RELATIONSHIP LANDSCAPE

I have read Martha (Beck), Brene (Brown), and Marianne (Williamson) in an attempt to improve my relationships, including the one with myself. With all the admiration I have for those ladies, I found myself overwhelmed when it came time to practice.

I appreciate the author's wisdom to filter the scientific research and present us a practical approach to mending relationships. Reading this book I felt the author's permission to be as curious as the Big Magic fans. I enjoyed the open-minded and straightforward words for their resemblance to the Buddhist monks' astuteness. With what I have learned from this book, I feel ready to face the questions I kept hiding from and get into action.

~ Andreea Munteanu, artist, author of *Why Is the Grass Green*

Navigating the Relationship Landscape is a masterpiece! What a great way to sit and reflect, looking at the beautiful pictures, carefully reading each section. This time of reflection allowed me to connect with my partner on a deeper level. This book is a game changer in relationships, it can be used again and again to empower the relationship!

~Kelly Walk, Author of *Memoirs of an Invisible Child*

Very inspiring and thought-provoking! It gives a feeling of hope that we can overcome our interpersonal challenges.
~ Rita Czarny, Family Mediator, 2mediateca.wordpress.com

A completely new to me, approach to self growth in an effort to improve relationships. If you want your relationships to work, it's up to your creativeness and ability to come up with solutions. This book helps you develop those skills. We all can use help and this book is a great and unique addition to our development.
~ Dr. Judson Somerville, www.vitamindblog.com

This book offers a fresh, compassionate, insightful and effective way to get in touch with what's really happening in any troubled relationship, lighting a path forward for change. And relief.
A thoughtful and thought-provoking book that's highly recommended for anyone who wants to understand herself (or himself) better, improve relationships and move from past pain to acceptance. And peace.
Also a useful tool appropriate for youth group/high school life skills courses and for counselors and therapists to use with their clients.
~ Jacquelyn Elnor Johnson, author of *Talk So He Will Listen: 12 Steps To Better Love Relationships for Women*, CrimsonHillBooks.com

This book is a unique collection of beautiful photos complemented with questions about life relationships. This body of work is the lens sweeping life in a 360 degree perspective. The section on the pillars of a great relationship was especially thought provoking.
This fine work reflects coach and bestselling author Gabriela Casineanu's artistic talent, poetic soul, and insightful perception of human relationships.
~ Lorraine Tong, author of *Hitler on Trial: Alan Cranston, Mein Kampf, and The Court of World Opinion*, LHTproductions.com

When I started reading this book I was not familiar with the Photo-Coaching concept, but by the end of it I found it appealing and easier to relate to the feelings generated by those images. The method can be applied to both personal and business relationship with certain adjustments. I've really enjoyed the read.
~ Claudiu Murgan, author of *The Decadence of Our Souls,* ClaudiuMurgan.com

There's great depth to 'Navigating the Relationship Landscape' that bares great fruit. Gabriela's questions through each chapter gives a realistic approach to the obstacles we all face in our relationships. Gabriela's message is solid throughout this read: To have greater relationships, you must adapt to that which is around you after you first grow within you.
~ Ryan Schoof, marketing consultant, speaker, writer

Visual images can connect deeply and powerfully with our subconscious desires, hopes and aspirations. That's the magical power of Gabriela Casineanu's uniquely creative Photo-Coaching books, and particularly 'Navigating the Relationship Landscape'.
All of us know how it feels to be caught in valued relationships that have turned stale—or angrily toxic. If you find yourself caught in that painful bind, this book can be the key to restoring the joy and love that has been lost. As a professional coach in personal development and leadership, I heartily recommend this book for its powerful simplicity, and deep insights. The pictures are compelling, and the text that accompanies each picture thought-provoking and truly liberating.
~ E. Thomas Behr, Ph.D., author of *The Tao of Sales: The Easy Way to Sell in Tough Times,* TomBehrBooks.com/the-tao-of-sales

≈

PRAISE FOR GABRIELA CASINEANU

Thank you for your guidance and support in a very difficult time in my life. Your expert coaching, exercises, photo-coaching book and other related tools unstuck me—helping me to realize my true potential and talents, and move forward. I'm now more focused, determined and confident about who I am, what is and is no longer important to me, what I want to achieve in my life and why. I feel well equipped to deal with anything that comes my way and ready to take it on!
~ Janette Burke, Marketing/PR coach

❧

It is amazing how Gabriela, through her ingenious combination of coaching methods, guided me patiently and wisely to blowing up my limiting beliefs and leading to the biggest discovery of my life: the awareness of my inner force and its unlimited potential. Previously I was seeing life as being hard, but thanks to her mastery, my perspective shifted: I find it now as an incredibly exciting and enjoyable journey. I consider myself fortunate for the moment when our destinies crossed and grateful for every moment we have spent together.
~ Mihaela Fecioru, HR Specialist

Gabriela is very intuitive and open-minded, which gives her great insight into understanding people on a deeper level. She has an excellent capacity to turn every situation into a self-discovery and learning opportunity, thus helping her clients come up with their own solutions. Moreover, by focusing on developing skills and teaching various techniques, she empowers and helps her clients learn how to be their own coach/therapist in the future. Overall, Gabriela is a great and inspiring coach!

~ Melania Lumezanu, B.A Psych., M. ADS

I was stunned to discover that my self-esteem was in time shattered by the negativities that surround me. It was still there, but not at the level I'd like it to be. I wasn't aware of these negativities and I didn't realize their impact on me. And who knows since when it lies there, hidden in a corner of my soul. Step by step, every coaching session increased my self-esteem, brought me the inner peace and answers to many problems. Frankly, I could say that I rediscovered myself, the one I used to be: enthusiastic and full of energy! Deft questions asked from the heart and with talent helped me to discover for myself the answers for each situation. Thanks, Gabriela!

~ Monica Brostean, Mechanical Engineer

I dedicate this book …

• *To you: I'm so happy you found it!*
The concepts from this book apply to any interpersonal relationship. I trust that you'll quickly discover their benefits in both your personal and professional life.
• *To those open to letting their relationships light up their path to self-growth.*
• *To those who don't like what I do: they too can learn something from this little book!*

To all … thank you!
Gabriela

Nothing is more exciting and bonding
in relationships than creating together.
~ Stephen R. Covey

How intentional are you about creating the relationship you want?

WHAT IS PHOTO-COACHING?

If you're already familiar with my first Photo-Coaching book (Meeting With My Self: Self-Coaching Questions That Invite Wisdom In), you can skip this chapter.

But if you're not, this is how the Photo-Coaching concept and this book series came to light:

Since I love nature and take lots of pictures, I occasionally noticed that some of them "speak" ... at least to me! :-)

In 2009, three years after I started my coaching practice, I began to feel frustrated that many people don't know what coaching is and what to expect from it. So I put together several "speaking" photos and the thoughts inspired by them, creating the first Photo-Coaching album ... as an invitation to self-reflection! I wanted to make *intangible coaching concepts* more *tangible* by combining visual elements with powerful coaching questions, to help people apply them in their own life.

Encouraged by the profound mindset shifts that

occurred in those who used the first Photo-Coaching album, in 2012 I created another one (about relationships). Soon after, life got in the way and I put this project aside.

Now I've been inspired to give it a new life as a series of published books. This way I can help more people while I focus on creating more books for the Photo-Coaching series (each designed around a specific theme).

As you probably noticed, I started to combine images and text even before Instagram was launched. :-)

Book 1
Meeting With My Self:
Self-Coaching Questions That Invite Wisdom In

This first book in the Photo-Coaching series is about you and your approach to life!

I've worked on myself a lot since 2006, and I can certainly see results. With this book, I invite you to go for ... a meeting with your own Self! If you like what you get the first time, you can come back to this book later on, anytime you need more answers, inspiration, or motivation.

If you wonder why you need such meetings with your Self, let me assure you that your inner world is connected with what you see happening in your life right now. On each page of *Meeting With Your Self* you'll find a combination of photographs and questions that invite you to engage in self-reflection, opening the door to a less explored place: your Inner World!

I hope this book and the next ones in this series will reveal more connections between your Inner and Outer Worlds.

Chapters 1 through 40 of *Meeting With Your Self* will help

you look at your situations from different perspectives, challenging your thinking, and helping you to see life from a more empowering point of view.

Now let's talk about Book 2:
Navigating the Relationship Landscape!

∼

ABOUT THIS BOOK

We cannot solve our problems with the same thinking we used when we created them.

— ALBERT EINSTEIN

The second book in the Photo-Coaching series—*Navigating the Relationship Landscape*—approaches an interpersonal relationship as a relationship System.

No two relationships we are a part of are the same, even if we're involved in both relationships. For example: your relationship with a colleague is different from the relationship you have with your mom... right?

You're the same person, but you probably bring different beliefs, attitudes and hopes to each relationship ... and these aspects can also evolve based on the events and interactions that will occur in time.

That's why in System Coaching we consider a relationship as a Relationship System (which is much more than the two people who are part of that relationship).

Looking at both personal and professional relationships

from this perspective allows us to bring a more intentional attitude toward any relationship we are a part of or will build in time.

~

Between 2007 and 2009, I was introduced to many interesting concepts (some illustrated in this book) through the advanced coaching training in Organizational and Relationship Systems Coaching (ORSC™) by CRR Global. Or System Coaching, as I like to say to make it easier.

Learning this type of coaching totally shifted my perspective about how I approach the relationships in my life.

And I hope this book will help you too!

To give you a brief idea: ORSC™ is based on *Systems Theory, Process Work, Family Systems Therapy, Alternative Dispute Resolution, Quantum Physics, Co-Active Coaching™*, and … *Taoism!*

This approach creates sustainable and resourceful relationship systems like teams, families, partnerships, friendships, etc.

At ORSC™ core is the study of the Relationship Systems Intelligence™.

As you can see, a lot of theory and scientific studies about relationships were considered in developing ORSC™.

I won't get into more details here … because I want this to be a practical book with immediate application to your relationships.

If you're interested in ORSC™, you can learn more from the book *Creating Intelligent Teams: Leading with Relationship Systems Intelligence*, by Anne Rød and Marita Fridjhon or from CRR Global.

I'll briefly mention that System Coaching (ORSC™) is also used to create more sustainable and resilient teams and organizations, but I plan to I'm explore this topic in a future book.

∾

Since I finished my ORSC™ training (2009), I started to use *System Thinking* and see *relationship systems* everywhere ... so I approached each of them from a System Coaching perspective!

∾

My first Photo-Coaching book (*Meeting With My Self*) applies the system thinking to the relationship we have ... with ourselves!

Many people go through life expecting more from others yet ignoring how they treat themselves—both physically and mentally.

No wonder that, in time, they disconnect from who they really are... gradually losing the connection with their own intuition!

The book *Meeting With My Self* is exactly about that; it's a tool that helps improve your relationship with yourself by decluttering the channel that connects with the intuition ... thus allowing your inner wisdom to help you overcome life's challenges and build a more meaningful life.

∾

This book *Navigating the Relationship Landscape* is meant to help you tap into the intelligence of a relationship (system) that you're a part of, to find solutions for overcoming your relationship challenges … and even build more meaningful relationships!

Some examples of where you can apply the concepts from this book: relationship with your partner, boss, colleague… your child, mother, friend …

The images from this book (which are my own photographs) and the related questions might have you thinking that I'm talking only about the relationship with a partner. But the concepts behind these questions are valid in other relationships as well (with a colleague, boss, parent, child, etc.). I trust that you can transfer them to other relationships you have because … they are transferable!

Things to ponder before you start going through this book:

• In System Coaching, we consider that in a relationship …. everyone is right but only partially! (from their perspective at least)

• As much as we want to, we can't change someone else's perspective, since it's based on years of experience and learning. What we can do is to help increase the person's awareness, which could lead—in time—to a perspective shift.

• That's what this book is about: to help you become more aware of the various aspects related to a relationship, so that you can see your relationships with different 'eyes.' It'll also equip you with *navigation tools* that help you prevent or overcome more easily a relationship's challenges.

• When you change the way you approach a relationship, or a particular situation, the other person's awareness will increase as well … potentially leading to a perspective shift on that side.

What you'll find inside

Each of the 40 chapters in this book will show you a combination of photographs and questions that invite you to reflection on a specific relationship or situation that you're going through.

This combination of visuals and self-reflection will help you look at the relationship (or the specific situation) from different angles, challenging your thinking, helping you to come up with ideas of what you can do differently to over-come the relationship challenges, and to create—more intentionally—the type of relationships you want.

If you're into personal development, rest assured that the relationships that come into your life are great triggers for self-growth! If you're open to that, this little book will also help you to learn more about yourself and how you can improve if you want more fulfilling relationships in your life!

∾

HOW TO USE THIS BOOK

An idea not coupled with action will never get any bigger than the brain cell it occupied.

— ARNOLD GLASOW

When you go through this book for the first time, pick a specific relationship you'd like to explore or a challenging relationship situation that you're going through.

The different chapters will invite you to put on new 'lenses' when you look at that specific relationship or situation.

I'm confident that you'll discover perspectives that you didn't previously consider, helping you to become more aware of what it is and what could be done differently in that specific situation or relationship … by respecting both the other and yourself!

Each of the 40 chapters is one to two pages long, each with a big image and coaching questions inviting self-reflection, opening the door to a less-explored *world*: the Relationship System!

If you expect this book to give you solutions, you'll be disappointed. Because no book alone can provide solutions to all relationship challenges.

What this book can do instead: it will help you get ideas and use new approaches to overcome your own relationships' challenges ... so you can take your relationships to the next level!

There's not much text (except Chapter 3), so it might look like an easy read. But the real power of this book consists in your experience with it: finding your own customized approach, based on your specific relationships and the challenges you encounter!

So your role will be to:

• Reflect on how the concepts and questions from each page apply to the relationship or situation you chose to reflect on.

• Take notes with the thoughts and ideas that came to your mind while exploring each chapter.

• Follow through with actions. As the quote above mentioned, you'll need to take action to see different results in your relationship.

It isn't complicated if you're really committed to see more positive changes... at least in your way to approach a relationship! But it can also lead to positive changes within the relationship.

~

If you like what you get the first time, come back to this book later on—anytime you need more motivation and inspiration on how to better approach a specific relationship or relationship challenge.

Let me know how it worked for you—either by leaving a

review for this book on Amazon, or by sending me a message (you'll find links at the end). Your feedback will help me understand what other books I can write to help more people like you.

∾

To start ...

Find a comfortable place, have a pen and notebook handy and get ready to start your *journey*.

Consider this book as a tool that facilitates the meeting between you and the relationship of your choice (or the situation you'd like to focus on).

You'll find below detailed instructions for ***first-time*** use. I highly recommend that you go through the entire book (Chapters 1-40) the first time, to get used to its style and see what you can expect from it.

Going through all the chapters will help you get many ideas of possible actions. Jot them down, prioritize, and use Post-it Notes as reminders to take those actions (or add them in your agenda). Without taking action, the desired changes will not occur!

Later on, come back to this book whenever you feel stressed or frustrated by a relationship, have a challenge or when you want new ideas on how to approach a specific relationship or challenge.

At that time, you might go quickly through some chapters, stopping only at those that resonate with you in the moment—as they might have something to *tell* you related to the topic you're exploring this time.

The process is similar to the first-time use, although fewer chapters may need to be revisited. Depending on the situation, you might resonate with different chapters each time you'll go again through the book.

After exploring this Photo-Coaching book for the first or second time, feel free to come up with other ways of using it.

For example: focus on one chapter per day or week or stay with a chapter until you've taken all the actions you came up with from the previous chapters.

$$\approx$$

Using this Photo-Coaching book for the **first time**

• *Start with Chapter 1*, where you are asked to choose a relationship you'd like to explore or improve. Make a note about it in your notebook. If you worry that someone will see your notes, use a symbol or word that reminds you what relationship you have in mind.

• *Clear your mind of any preconceived ideas* and allow yourself to be curious. Start with beginner's mind!

• *Go chapter by chapter and answer the questions* provided, or take time to reflect on each topic. Jot down the ideas you come up with based on each chapter's content. Also, write down the actions you could take in that specific relationship or situation.

• After you go through all chapters: *prioritize* the ideas and actions generated based on the importance and urgency: what needs to be addressed first to keep things from getting worse. Sometimes important things might not seem urgent, but putting them aside for too long can affect the relationship.

• *Write the actions with a higher rank* on Post-it Notes, give them *due dates*, and place them in areas you visit frequently. They will remind you to take those actions. If Post-it Notes don't work for you, choose something else (it has to be something physical: paper agenda, phone calendar/alarm, etc). Believing that you'll remember later might not work because your list of ideas and actions will soon disappear from focus when you get back to your busy life.

• *Take action!* Without taking the these actions your good intentions won't be enough to improve the relationship or a specific situation!

• *Don't get discouraged* if your actions don't seem to have an immediate effect. Remember what I said about increased awareness leading to a perspective shift? Unless people know how to positively shift their perspective (and many don't), it might take time until the desired results become visible.

• *Notice your progress* and *celebrate your successes*, even the small ones! (like getting the courage to complete an action)

Now grab your pen and notebook, and let's get started!

1

INTENTION

If there is a better way to deal with relationships, which relationship* would you choose to improve?

*Pick one relationship for now. You can always come back to this book later to explore another relationship.

2

SEPARATE ENTITY

Two waves together create a new pattern,
which has a different behavior.

In the same way, the relationship between people
is a separate entity (different from the people themselves).

How can you nurture your relationship
to shape the pattern the way you want?

PILLARS

Some of the essential **pillars*** of any great relationship:
Collaboration, Playfulness, Gratitude, Being Present,
Commitment, Democracy, Inquiry/Awareness, Respect.

Which one is your strength?
What is your weakness?
How can your strength help you improve your weakness?

Collaboration   Inquiry/Awareness   Being Present   Respect   Commitment   Gratitude   Democracy   Playfulness

*The pillars that sustain a relationship, the way I describe them:

Collaboration

Without it, there's no real relationship. By encouraging more collaboration, while keeping in mind your relationship's common goal, you can build a better relationship. Leveraging your strengths could also play an important role in a successful collaboration.

Don't yet know what's your common goal? Having a discussion about that will help you get on the same page and put things in perspective when things get hard.

Inquiry/Awareness

Asking questions can help you both better understand the situation and what's going on in the relationship. More fitting solutions could spring out of learning each other's point of view on the situation—instead of ignoring or guessing.

Just avoid questions that start with "why" if it's about a current or past situation. Such questions put people on the defensive, which is one of the negative behaviors that could affect a relationship.

Yet "why" questions are excellent when it comes to future situations. They motivate people by helping them to connect with the meaningful reason behind the desired situation.

Being Present

By consciously staying present to whatever happens in the moment (instead of tuning out), you're more prone to handle that situation well.

If you're able to notice when someone tunes out (thinking about something else or simply avoiding full participation)... so can the other person! Which is often perceived as lack of interest in dealing with that specific situation. Not the best way to overcome a relationship challenge, right?

Respect

When it comes to relationships, people might have different definitions for respect. Have you discussed what it means for each of you?

There are two aspects to consider:

• Respect for the other: That each of you is naturally creative, resourceful, and whole

• Respect for yourself: If you don't respect yourself, why would you expect someone else to? This also includes allowing your voice to be heard instead of letting the other person guess what you think or feel.

Commitment

This pillar is similar to saying you respect the relationship and you're committed to helping it achieve, in time, its purpose. If only one of you (or neither) cares, the relationship is left at the mercy of the internal and external factors which can ruin it if the commitment doesn't hold it together.

Gratitude/Intentional Appreciation

By focusing on the positives (good moments from your past, the other's admirable traits, etc.), you infuse positive energy into the relationship. The "magic ratio" is 5 to 1 (positive to negative), according to Dr. Gottman who conducted over 40 years of breakthrough research in this field.

Deep Democracy/Diversity

This pillar is about inviting the others to voice and respect their opinions. It opens up the space to better understand what's going on.

Some people might have a negative way of expressing their opinions, but there might be reasons behind that behavior that—once understood—might open up the situation to a better way of overcoming the challenge.

Others prefer not to speak up—yet, their opinion counts too. It might be the missing element to the *puzzle*. Encouraging them to speak, by helping them understand the value of their opinion, leads to better solutions.

Playfulness

Last but not least is the ability to not take yourself too seriously. Your opinion counts but it's based only on your perspective.

Being open to listening the other person's opinion and even bringing some lightness to the discussion goes a long way in building a more enjoyable relationship.

～

Are there pillars missing in the relationship you're exploring?
What can you do to have them present more often in your relationship?

4

"WINTER"

There could be "winter" moments in your relationship.
But with strong pillars built over time,
your relationship can hold on until "spring" is back.

5

DECISION

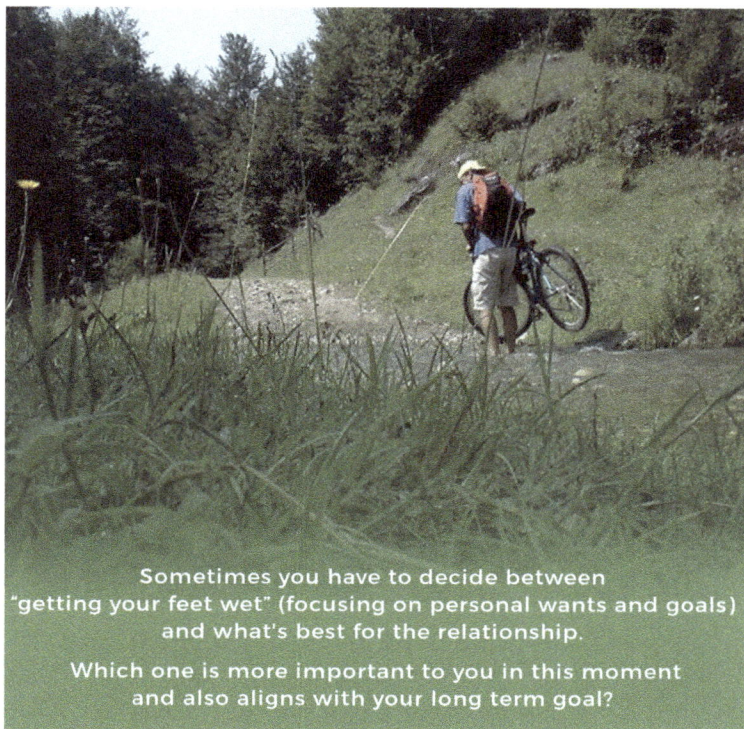

Sometimes you have to decide between
"getting your feet wet" (focusing on personal wants and goals)
and what's best for the relationship.

Which one is more important to you in this moment
and also aligns with your long term goal?

13

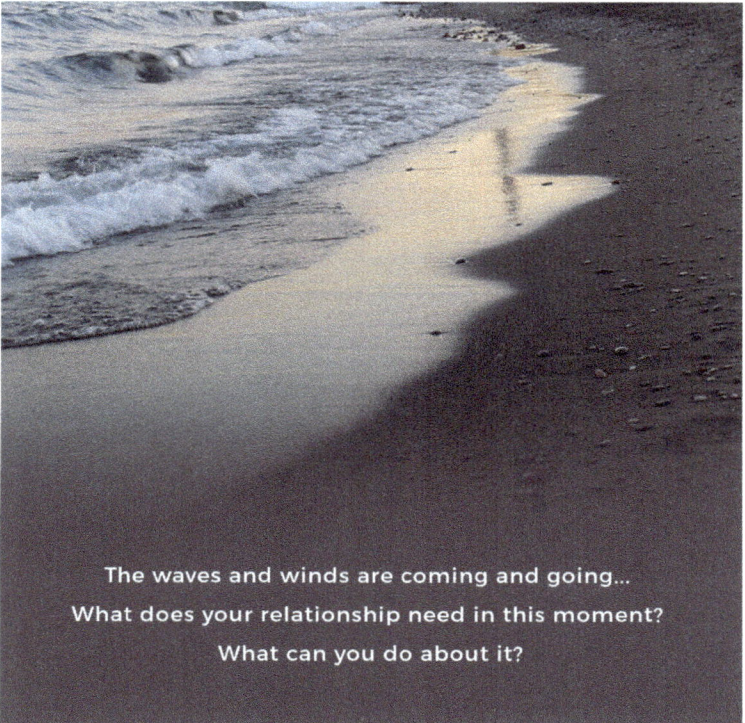

6

WAVES

The waves and winds are coming and going...
What does your relationship need in this moment?
What can you do about it?

7

ENJOY

Ohhh... vacations!

Do you really have to wait until both of you have time for a longer vacation?

Or you could find here and there moments to enjoy yourselves together (or even by yourself)?

These moments could recharge your batteries to continue the journey.

There might be times when you decide the other way.

8

LEAD?

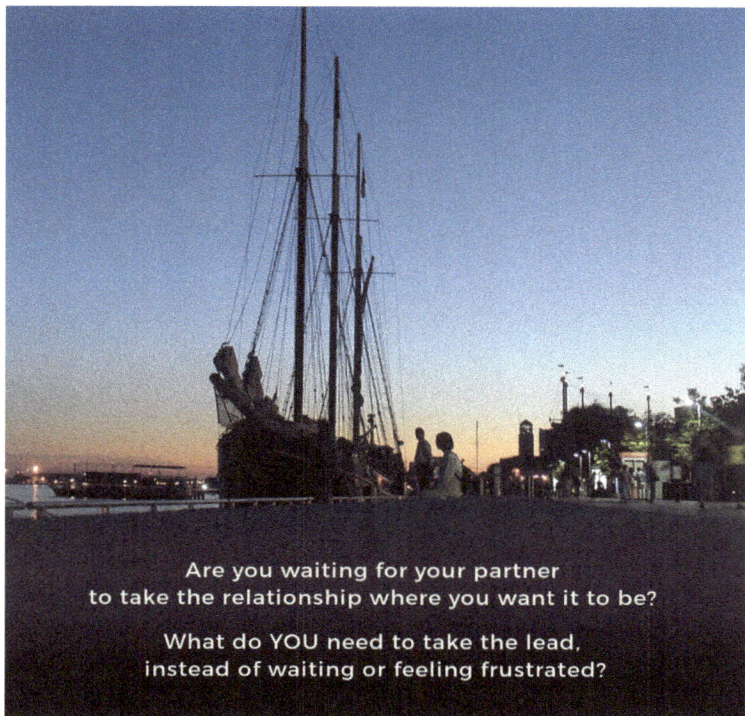

Are you waiting for your partner
to take the relationship where you want it to be?

What do YOU need to take the lead,
instead of waiting or feeling frustrated?

9

SPEAK UP

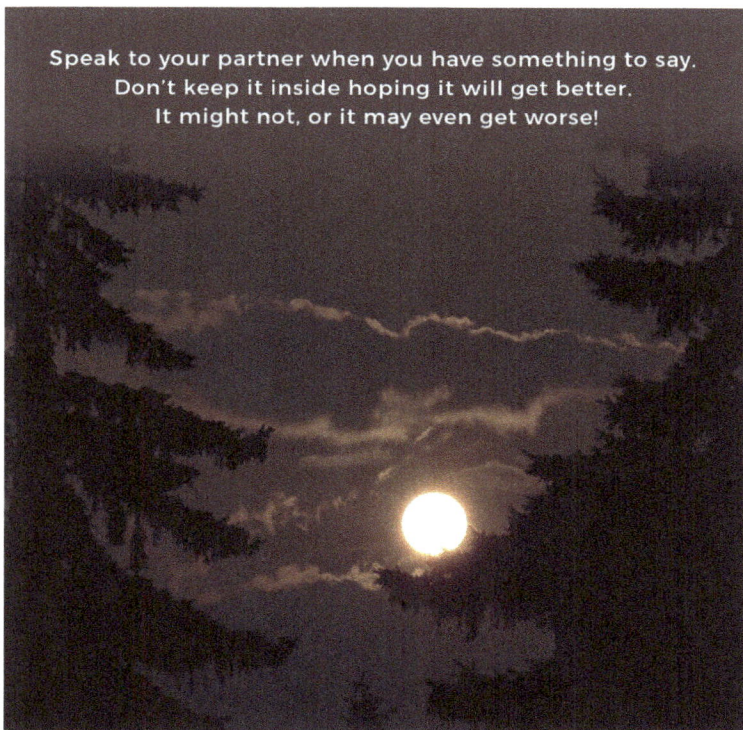

Speak to your partner when you have something to say.
Don't keep it inside hoping it will get better.
It might not, or it may even get worse!

10

TAKE A BREAK

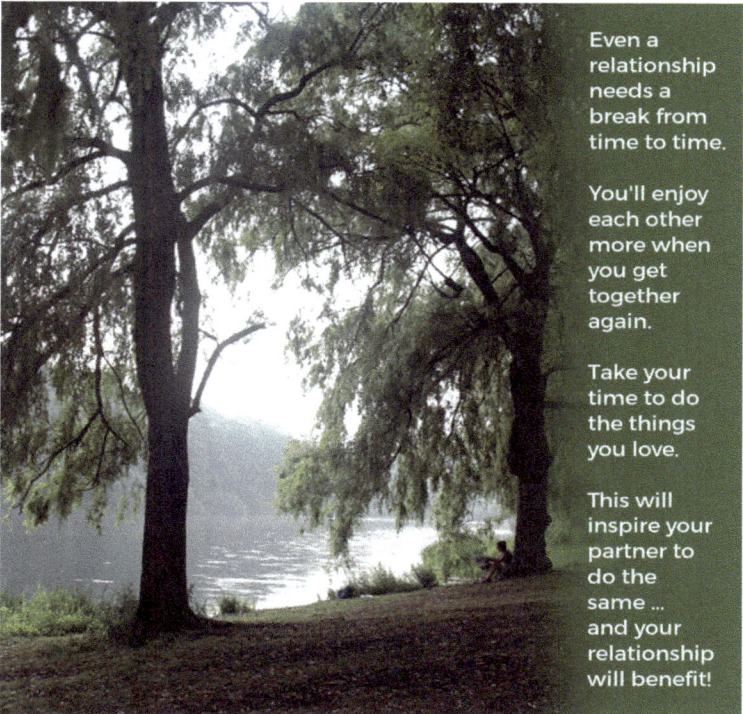

Even a relationship needs a break from time to time.

You'll enjoy each other more when you get together again.

Take your time to do the things you love.

This will inspire your partner to do the same ... and your relationship will benefit!

11

PLAYFULNESS

Taking yourself too
seriously might hurt
the relationship.

Your opinion
might be only your
perspective about
the situation!

How can you have a
lighter approach to
your discussions
without becoming a
clown?

PS: In a relationship,
everyone is right
but only partially!

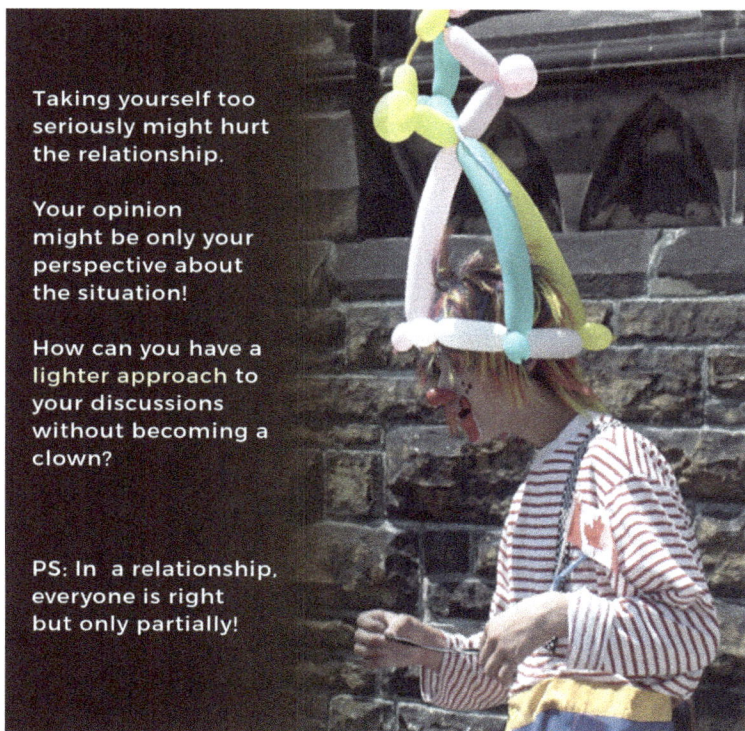

12

CELEBRATE

A successful day?
Learned
something new?
New job?
...

Celebrate!
It doesn't have
to be a big fest.

Anything works,
as long as you
get into a
celebratory
mood!

This gives you
energy to
continue and
reconnect with
the feeling of
fulfillment!

13

GAP

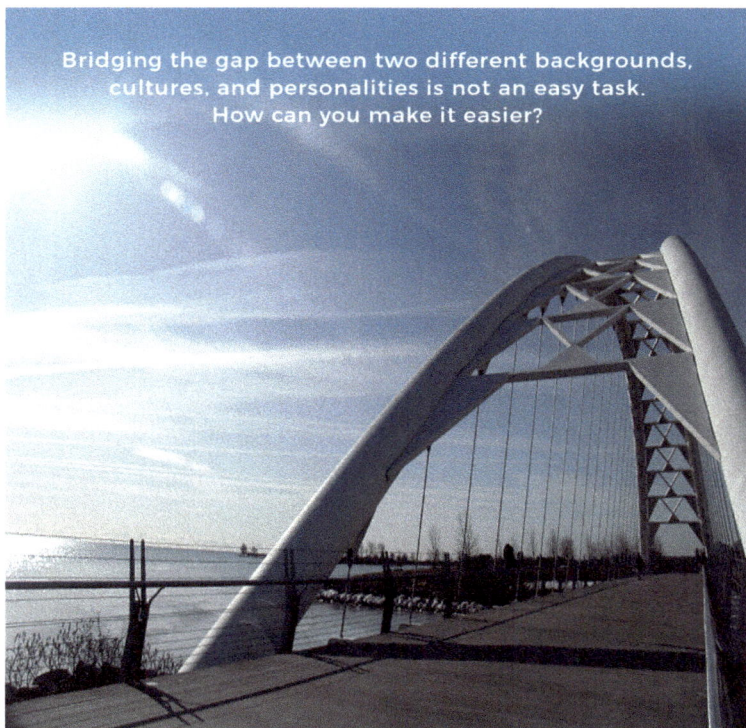

Bridging the gap between two different backgrounds, cultures, and personalities is not an easy task. How can you make it easier?

14

CHALLENGE

Facing a challenge?

Get together with your partner as a team
and define strategies to overcome it.
No need to face it by yourself!

Even the relationship gets stronger through collaboration!

RUNNING AWAY

"Running away" from a situation might not be the best solution.

How else can you handle it?

NEW DIRECTION

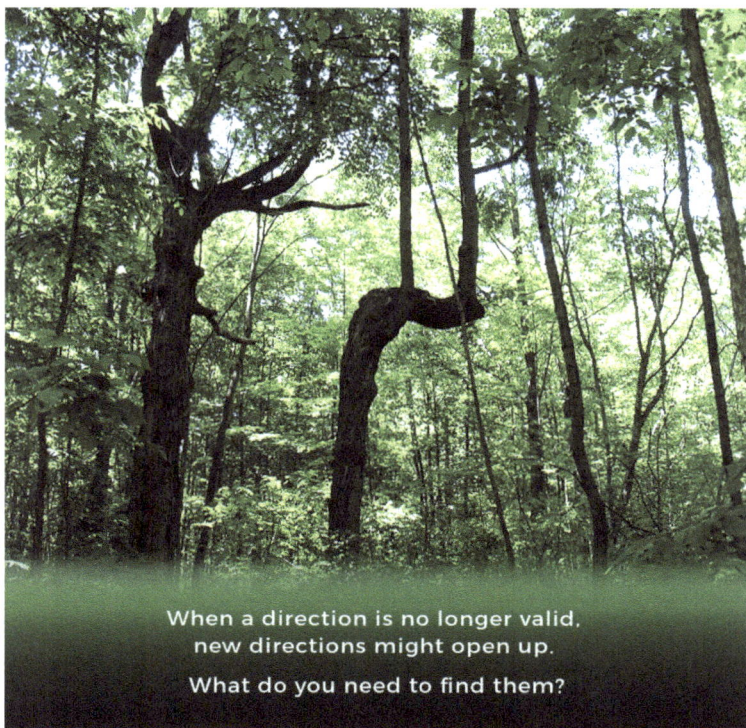

When a direction is no longer valid,
new directions might open up.

What do you need to find them?

META-RELATIONSHIP

A meta-relationship has a common direction established together, that benefits both partners and the entire world. And they adjust their path accordingly.

If you want to create a meta-relationship, what could help you get there?

18

NEW

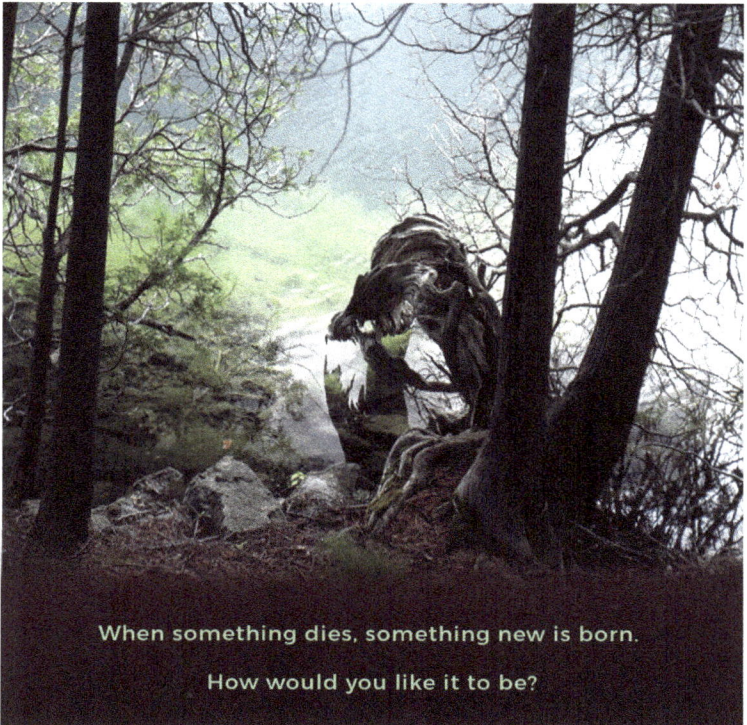

When something dies, something new is born.

How would you like it to be?

19

ENVIRONMENT

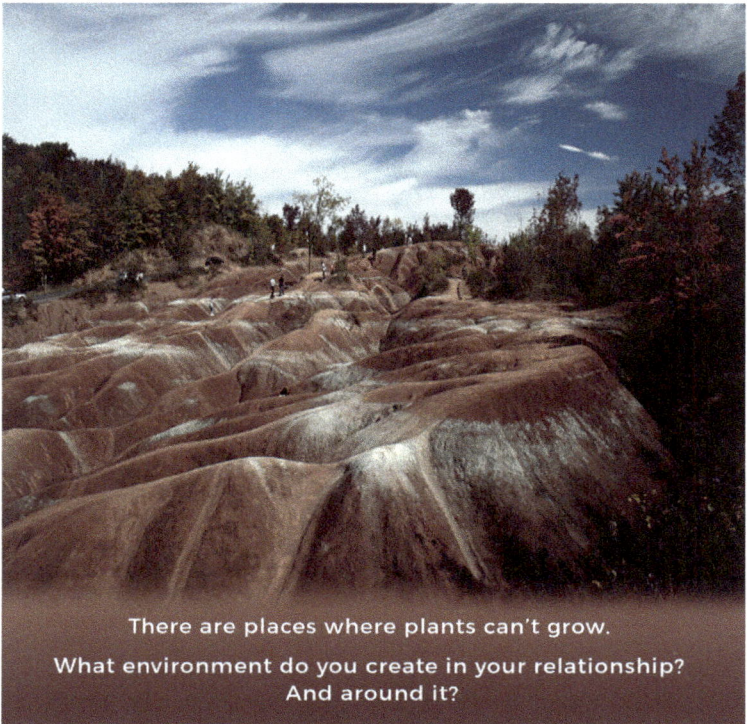

There are places where plants can't grow.

What environment do you create in your relationship?
And around it?

20

IDEAS

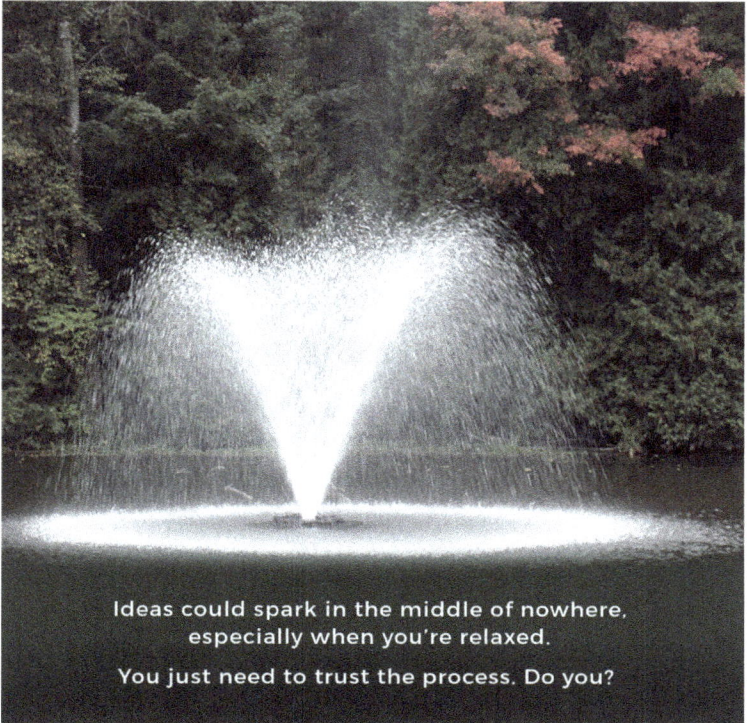

Ideas could spark in the middle of nowhere,
especially when you're relaxed.

You just need to trust the process. Do you?

STRENGTHS

Feeling sometimes that everything falls apart?

What are your relationship's strengths to hang on to?

On which of your strengths can you rely on?

SIDE BY SIDE

Do you feel left behind?

What do you need
to stand up and
"walk" together?

Ask yourself
and your partner:

What do you need
to go side by side
in the same direction?

ABRASIVE

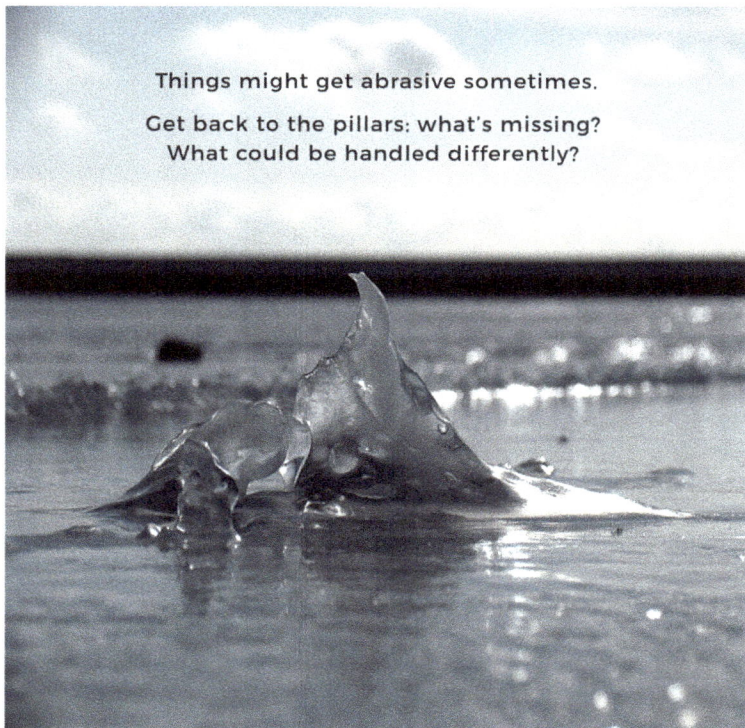

Things might get abrasive sometimes.

Get back to the pillars: what's missing?
What could be handled differently?

24

STEPPING BACK

Do you get upset when your partner
steps back from what s/he said?

Get curious instead!
There might be a valid reason behind that action.

25

WARMTH

The warmth of your heart could **light up** the most difficult moments.

Reach out and show it, don't let your partner guess if you still have it or not.

You don't need to wait for difficult moments... to show the warmth of your heart!

26

FOUR TOXINS

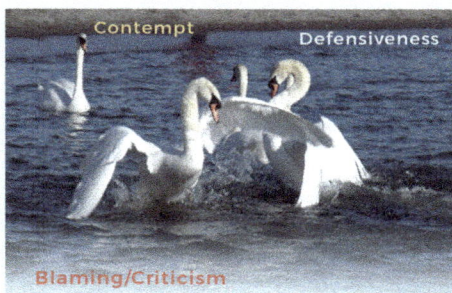

These four
negative
behaviors
could destroy
any relationship!

Notice when they
show up in your
relationship.

How can you avoid
using them yourself?

How do you handle it
when they are used
by your partner?

SEEDS

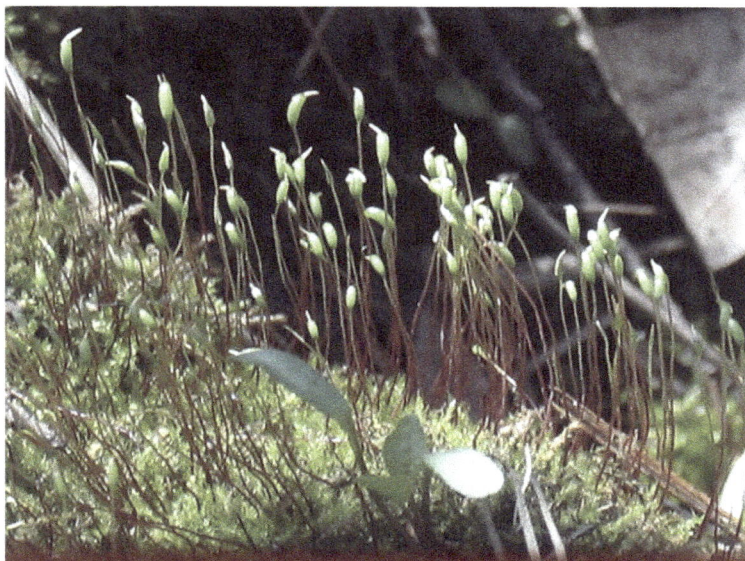

Today's "seeds" are tomorrow's "fruits."

What fruits would you like from your relationship?
What kind of relationship would you like to create?
What seeds do you need to plant for that?

28

HAPPINESS

Everyone wants happiness and success.

Discuss together what these mean to each of you
and how can you help each other to get there.

Otherwise, misunderstanding could kick in
and you might not get what you want.

29

POSITIVITY

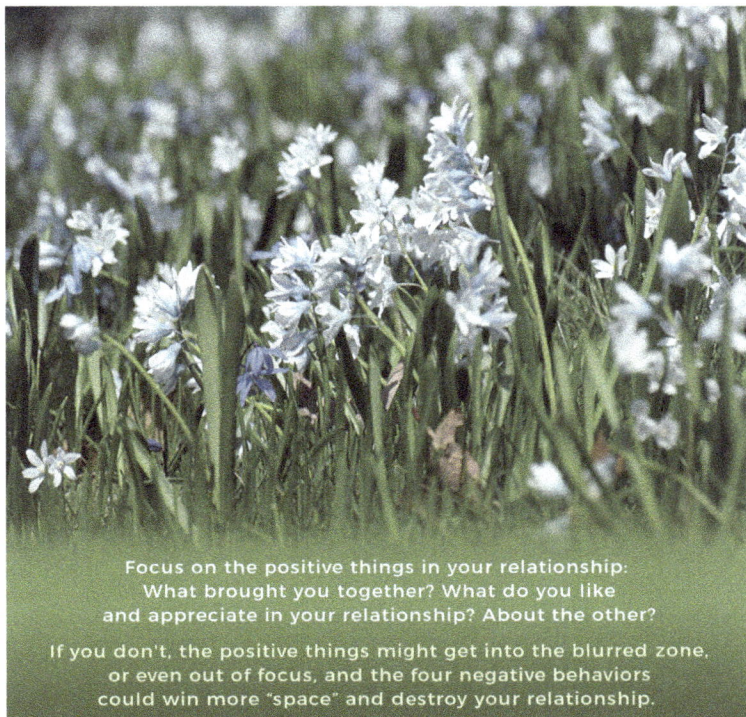

Focus on the positive things in your relationship:
What brought you together? What do you like
and appreciate in your relationship? About the other?

If you don't, the positive things might get into the blurred zone,
or even out of focus, and the four negative behaviors
could win more "space" and destroy your relationship.

30

DIRECTION

It's ok if sometimes
your personal directions
are not the same,
as long as you agree on
the relationship's direction
and follow through.

CHANGE

How do you approach
the change that just
occurred in your
relationship?
(job loss, career
change, move to new
house, new child, etc.)

It will certainly affect
your relationship and
the roles* you
previously defined
for each of you.

What roles would you
like to focus on now?

Which ones do you
want to maintain or
change, and how?

*You *play* concurrent roles in parallel, though some have competing priorities. For example: being a wife, daughter, mother, employee, friend ...

When a change occurs, our roles and priorities in a relationship might need to change. Revisiting and readjusting the roles in a relationship can prevent role nausea or poorly occupied roles in the future—leading to less frustration and conflict.

32

"PHANTOMS"

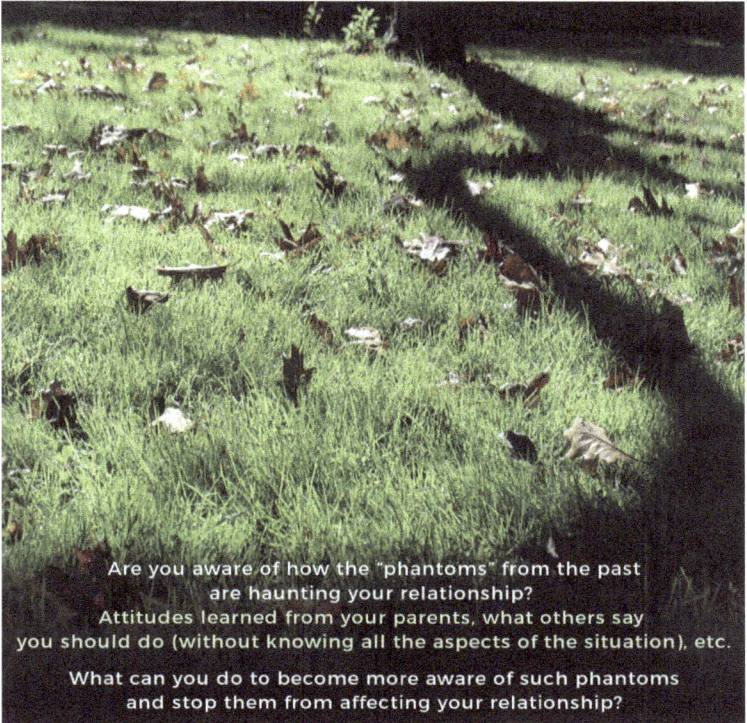

Are you aware of how the "phantoms" from the past
are haunting your relationship?
Attitudes learned from your parents, what others say
you should do (without knowing all the aspects of the situation), etc.

What can you do to become more aware of such phantoms
and stop them from affecting your relationship?

33

EMOTIONS

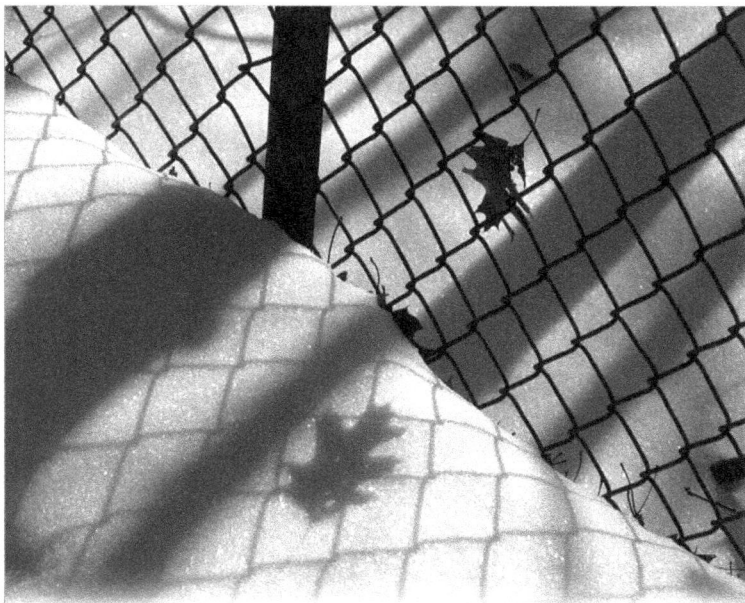

Holding on to emotions from past experiences could affect
your relationship: guilt, resentment, frustration, anger, fear ...
Learn from the past and let it go!
Focus on doing your best in every present moment.

"CONSTRUCTION"

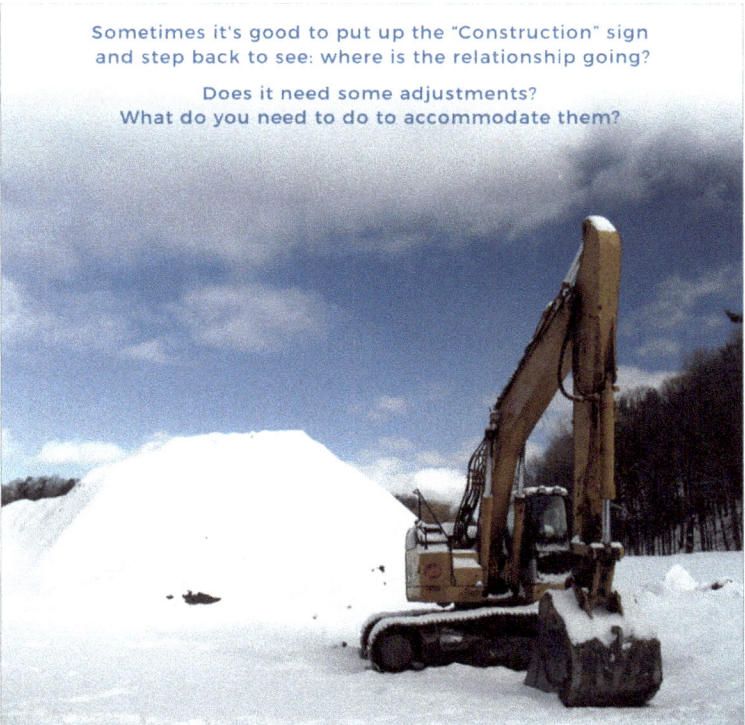

Sometimes it's good to put up the "Construction" sign
and step back to see: where is the relationship going?

Does it need some adjustments?
What do you need to do to accommodate them?

35

DRAIN

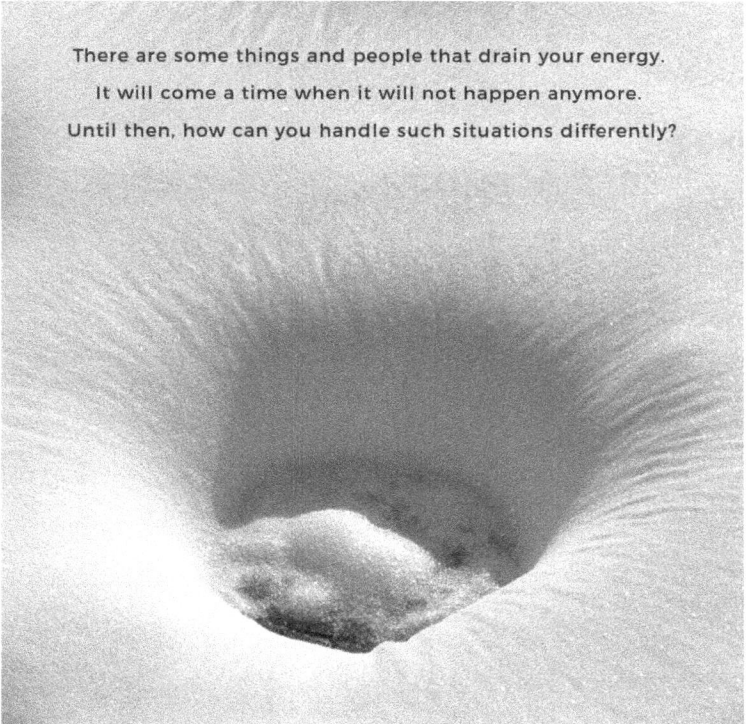

There are some things and people that drain your energy.
It will come a time when it will not happen anymore.
Until then, how can you handle such situations differently?

NEW ADVENTURES

You might get to a point when you feel that you're ready to "fly" to new adventures, but the relationship is holding you back.

In this case, did you open up to your partner to understand where you both "are"?

Did you learn your own lessons?*

*Relationships have the potential to help us grow. Those aspects that we don't like in others show up because they resonate with something inside us that needs to be healed (it might be something we're not aware of because it's deeply hidden in our subconscious).

Leaving a relationship without healing those inner aspects might attract in your life other people with a similar behavior you try to avoid. This process can become a pattern that affects one relationship after another, until the healing occurs.

Self-growth also helps the healing, while coaching can accelerate this process.

37

PAST - FUTURE

There are people who are afraid of the future,
and feel guilty or regret the past.
Are you one of them?
Thinking too much about the future or the past
diminishes your ability to enjoy the present moment.
Find the beauty and positivity around you and in your relationship,
and the future will unfold by itself in the same manner.

38

GRATEFULNESS

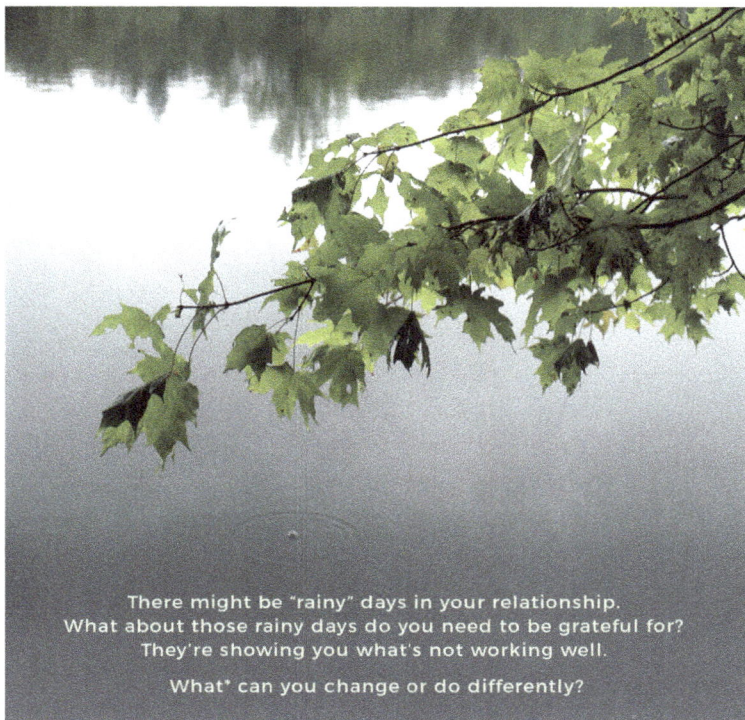

There might be "rainy" days in your relationship.
What about those rainy days do you need to be grateful for?
They're showing you what's not working well.

What* can you change or do differently?

* *Nothing* is not a valid answer if you don't want more *rainy* days in your relationship.

BOUNDARIES

Are you aware of your own boundaries?
Did you set some for yourself?
Do you let others know what you're willing to accept
and what you're not?

THERE'S MORE …

There's much more about navigating the relationship landscape
and how to handle specific situations.
Curious to learn more?
Start by applying what you've learned here first.
And if you still want more, you can reach out to me.

AFTERWORD

The time for action is now.
It's never too late to do something.
~ Antoine de Saint-Exupery

Although I could add more chapters to this book, I was inspired to end it here. I will come back with other books in the Photo-Coaching series.

It seems natural to end the book with the question "Curious to learn more?" because a lot of people are eager to learn more once you spark their curiosity… yet, they forget to put first in practice what they learned.

Real change occurs when we develop new behaviors, not when we just become aware of them. Especially in a relationship, it takes practice to integrate a new behavior and build credibility for your new attitude.

For me, the relationships that life brings me are like a mirror that reflects back to me how I am. There are aspects that I like, and that's great. But the ones I don't… open the door to self-discovery and improvement! I recently went through a professional relationship that taught me the lesson of patience and showed me the benefits of maintaining integrity with myself (no matter what other would think or say).

This makes me consider life as a self-discovery journey and using coaching questions like the ones in this book help this process.

That's why I created this book as a self-coaching guide, to help you ... help your relationships!

~

Thank you for reading *Navigating the Relationship Landscape!*

I hope that it adds value and quality to your life, and you'll come back to it when you need more ideas on how to improve your relationships.

Please leave a review for this book; your feedback will help others make a more informed decision when considering buying this book. And who knows, maybe your review will also help others discover this book and positively impact their relationships!

It will also help me improve my writing craft and understand how the books in the Photo-Coaching series can be improved.

Let's build a better world together for all of us!

All the best,

Gabriela Casineanu

~

If you'd like to get notified I publish new books:
GabrielaCasineanu.com/series

ABOUT THE AUTHOR

Gabriela Casineanu has successfully navigated many life challenges and career transitions. She started her professional life in engineering, later on adding entrepreneurship, coaching, art, and writing … continuing to explore life with the curiosity of a child!

She is a certified Professional Coach by the International Coach Federation (2008), and was trained by two prestigious coaching training schools: CTI (Co-Active Coaching) and CRR Global (Organization & Relationship Systems Coaching).

With a daily meditation practice and a passion for self-discovery, she relies on intuition to guide her next steps.

Reflecting on her own path, Gabriela Casineanu writes books that would have liked to find to help her navigate life more easily.

GabrielaCasineanu.com
gabriela.casineanu@gmail.com

Instagram: @ThoughtsDesigner
Facebook: GC.ThoughtsDesigner
Twitter: @thoughtdesigner
LinkedIn: gabrielacasineanu
Amazon.com/author/gabrielacasineanu

ALSO BY GABRIELA CASINEANU

BOOKS

GabrielaCasineanu.com/book

Although grouped by themes, all books are stand-alone.

Introverts Strengths Series

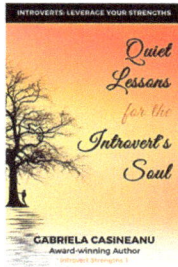

Job Search/Career Series

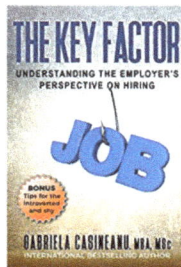

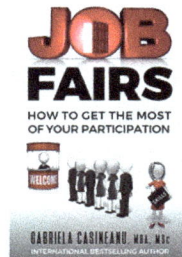

Photo-Coaching Series (self-coaching)

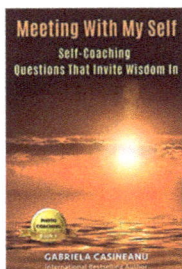

Meeting With My Self
Self-Coaching
Questions That Invite Wisdom In

GABRIELA CASINEANU
International Bestselling Author

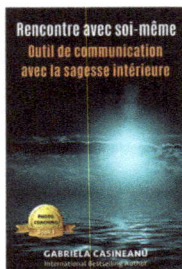

Rencontre avec soi-même
Outil de communication
avec la sagesse intérieure

GABRIELA CASINEANU
International Bestselling Author

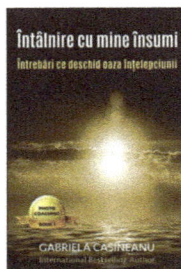

Întâlnire cu mine însumi
Întrebări ce deschid oara înțelepciunii

GABRIELA CASINEANU
International Bestselling Author

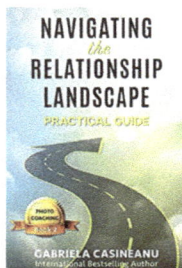

NAVIGATING *the* **RELATIONSHIP LANDSCAPE**
PRACTICAL GUIDE

GABRIELA CASINEANU
International Bestselling Author

RELATIONS HARMONIEUSES
Carte routière
pour naviguer avec aisance

GABRIELA CASINEANU
International Bestselling Author

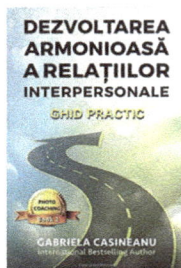

DEZVOLTAREA ARMONIOASĂ A RELAȚIILOR INTERPERSONALE
GHID PRACTIC

GABRIELA CASINEANU
International Bestselling Author

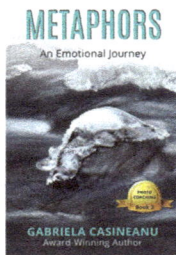

METAPHORS
An Emotional Journey

GABRIELA CASINEANU
Award-Winning Author

UPCOMING BOOKS: GabrielaCasineanu.com/series

COACHING/ SPEAKING: GabrielaCasineanu.com/contact

ACKNOWLEDGMENTS

Many thanks to all who contributed to helping me understand the world through a more empowering perspective:

• Marita Fridjhon and Faith Fuller, the co-founders of the Organizational and Relationships Systems Coaching (ORSC™)—training delivered by CRR Global worldwide.

• My System Coaching colleagues and clients who helped me gain the experience and expertise in this advanced coaching niche that has the potential to impact millions

• All those who believe in and support me in this exciting self-discovery journey that allows me to explore life with fresh new eyes

• And … those like you, who are curious to learn and explore new perspectives that could enrich their lives!

❧

BIBLIOGRAPHY

• Anne Rød and Marita Fridjhon, *Creating Intelligent Teams: Leading with Relationship Systems Intelligence*, (KR Publishing, 2013)
• *Organization and Relationship Systems Coaching* (ORSC™): https://www.crrglobal.com/orsc.html
• Kyle Benson, *The Magic Relationship Ratio, According to Science*: https://www.gottman.com/blog/the-magic-relationship-ratio-according-science/
• Dr. John Gottman: https://www.gottman.com/about/john-julie-gottman/

www.ingramcontent.com/pod-product-compliance
Lightning Source LLC
Chambersburg PA
CBHW041216030426
42336CB00023B/3360